Vision 2

Values for Life

Collins

Vision 2

Values for Life

Published by Collins Learning
A division of Harper*Collins* Publishers India Private Limited

HarperCollins *Publishers*
A-75, Sector 57, Noida, Uttar Pradesh 201301, India

1 London Bridge Street, London, SE1 9GF, United Kingdom
2 Bloor Street East, Toronto, Ontario M4W 1A8, Canada

Lvl 13, 201 Elizabeth Street (PO Box A565, NSW, 1235), Sydney NSW 2000, Australia

195 Broadway, New York, NY 10007, USA

Browse the complete Collins catalogue at **www.collins.in**

For any queries/feedback, please write to us at ***SCHOOLSUPPORT@harpercollins.co.in*** *or call us on* ***0120-4044800***

First published in 2016
Latest reprint edition *2020*

Reprint: 10

ISBN: 978-93-5136-902-8

Content designed and developed by
Sutapa Basu and Henu Mehtani

Artwork and layout by
Henu Studio Private Limited

Printed and bound in India by Thomson Press India Ltd.

Acknowledgements

Cover: Henu Studio Private Limited

Acknowledgements are due to the following for permission to use copyright content:

Sutapa Basu for Grandfather's Little Mother

Preface

Vision—Values for life is an engaging value education series meant to enable learners lead a balanced, happy and successful life. The National Curriculum Framework states that education must reflect the values, structure and beliefs to equip young learners with a holistic personality. This series encourages learners to respect diversity, exhibit leadership, display positive attitude towards community and the nation, and be responsible and strive for conflict management in stressful situations. Focusing on the self, the community and the nation, this series guides learners to develop co-scholastic aspects of their personality, namely, life skills, attitude and values.

The social dynamics in the recent past have ushered in consumerist tendencies the world over, impacting our lifestyles and attitudes. Youngsters today are restless due to their inability to cope with changing life patterns, expectations and comparisons with peers. *Vision* intends to equip the learners with relevant emotional skills and competencies to deal with difficult situations by presenting examples from real life.

Vision follows an interactive approach, and caters for all kinds of learners with different learning styles. Values are presented through progressively graded stories, anecdotes or poems. Young children learn by doing, hence the series has a variety of hands-on activities, encouraging quiet reflection and sound action.

Discuss, a warm-up exercise, introduces the chapter and **Relate** gives real-life situations for application-based assessment. **Think and Say** poses problem-solving situations to encourage lateral thinking. **Workout** gives interesting activities to reinforce the values and **Create** provides a creative activity to strengthen the concept. **Enjoy** provides fun activities to help learners imbibe the values. **Be smart** has exercises based on multiple intelligences to ensure overall development of the learners. **Life Skills** activity pages have colouring and fun tasks to reinforce important skills required to excel in life, and **Projects** provide engaging value-based tasks for the young learners.

Vision hopes to encourage the learners to imbibe the right values and attitudes that would make them good human beings.

Contents

Detailed Contents

Key Elements

Discuss
Warm-up exercise for students to become familiar with the mood of the chapter

Read along
A story or poem related to the value being discussed in the chapter

Figure out
Questions based on the Read along section which aims at testing the understanding of the value taught

Relate
Situations to test the application of the value taught

Workout
Interesting worksheets that reinforce the value taught

Create
Creative activity that is a fun way to strengthen the concept of the value

Remember
Brief pointers that the students can incorporate in their behaviour

Enjoy
Suggests media that communicates the value discussed

Be smart
Exercises based on multiple intelligences to ensure overall development of the learner

Life Skills
Activity sheets based on different life skills to help learn these skills

Project
Practical projects based on the values taught in the book

Problem Solving Assessment: Questions related to the value highlighted in the chapter encouraging students to think laterally

Think and Say

Your alarm clock has stopped working. How can you still wake up on time?

Tips for teachers to take the lesson forward

Teaching tips

- Bring out the various ways in which people appear to be unequal.

1. Ali Runs for Rules

Discuss

Look at the pictures. Talk about them in class.

Read along

Ali's grandfather is not well. He is in the hospital.

Ali's father is going to visit him.

'May I come too, Father?' asks Ali.

'But don't you have your football practice today?' asks Father.

'You can drop me at the football field after we meet Grandfather,' says Ali.

While driving, Father's mobile starts ringing. Father moves the car to the side of the road and stops. Then he talks on his phone.

When he finishes the call, Ali asks, 'Father, why did you stop the car to take the call?'

Father replies, 'This is a rule we follow while driving on the road. If we talk on the phone while driving, we cannot drive safely.'

When they reach the hospital, they stand in a queue to get an entry pass.

'Why can't we just go inside?' asks Ali.

Father replies, 'Because, we need to follow the rules of the hospital.'

After meeting Grandfather, Father drives Ali to the football field.

Father stops at the traffic light as it turns red.

Think and Say

It is a rule to keep wet umbrellas outside the classroom on a rainy day. One rainy morning, your teacher is not in class. What will you do with your wet umbrella?

'Father, I will be late for my practise. Please drive through,' Ali requests.

'No Ali! Traffic rules are for our own safety,' says Father. 'If I drive through the red light, I'll be breaking the rules of the road. If I break the rules of the road, there might be an accident,' he explains.

Ali understands that rules are very important.

He reaches the football field ten minutes late.

'Ali, you are late. Run around the field,' says the football coach.

'Now Ali, do you understand why rules are important?' asks Dad, looking at Ali.

'Yes, Father!' says Ali with a smile. He begins his run.

Father smiles too.

Figure out

Tick (✓) the correct options to complete the sentences.

1. Ali's father stops the car on the side of the road to talk on his phone because
   a. it is not safe to drive while talking on the phone. ☐
   b. a policeman asks him to stop. ☐
2. Father waits in queue to get an entry pass at the hospital because
   a. he is afraid of the hospital guard. ☐
   b. it is a hospital rule to get an entry pass to enter the hospital. ☐
3. Father stops at the traffic light because
   a. someone may get hurt if he breaks this traffic rule. ☐
   b. a traffic policeman was looking at Father. ☐

4. Ali has to run around the field because
   a. he is late for practise. ☐
   b. he likes running. ☐
5. Father smiles when Ali runs around the field because
   a. he wants his son to run. ☐
   b. he knows that Ali understands that rules are important for everyone. ☐

Relate

Choose the best answer. Draw a smiley ☺ against it.

1. You have brushed your teeth at night but you feel like eating an ice cream from the fridge. What would you do?

a. Eat the ice cream and then brush your teeth again

b. Eat the ice cream and go to bed without brushing your teeth

2. You are in the school library and are reading a funny book. What would you do?

a. Laugh quietly, so you do not disturb others

b. Laugh out loud

3. You finish your packet of wafers in the car. What would you do with the empty pack?

a. Throw it in a dustbin when you spot one

b. Throw it on the road

Create

Do this activity in class. Each of you should follow the instructions to make a Rule Placard. Share your rule with the class.

You need

- A long, strong stick
- A quarter sheet of chart paper
- Adhesive tape
- Bold markers

Steps

1. Write 'Playground Rule' on top of the paper.
2. Write any one rule that you would follow on the playground.
3. Using the adhesive tape, attach the chart paper to the stick.
4. Your Rule Placard is ready. Share your rule with the class.

Remember

Home rules

- Eat your meals on time.
- Follow a timetable for your daily routine.
- Leave home only after you have asked your elders.

School rules

- Follow the timetable.
- Make a queue wherever it is needed.
- Maintain silence in your class and library.

Road rules

- Cross the road at the zebra crossing.
- Never go alone on the road.
- Wear a seat belt when you are in a car and a helmet when on a bike.

Enjoy

Watch a match of your favourite sport on the TV and see how the rules are followed.

Be smart

While playing any game or sport, we need to wear the right clothes or use the right things to play. Match the sports with what we need to play them with.

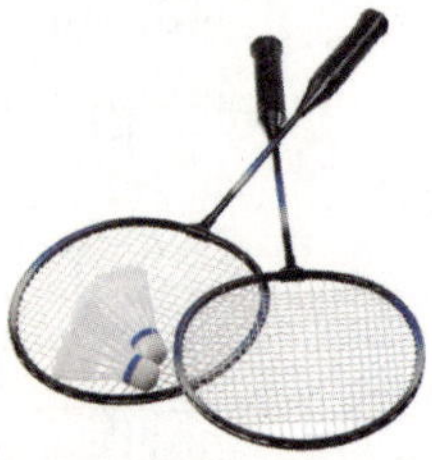

Swimming
Badminton
Cycling
Football
Cricket

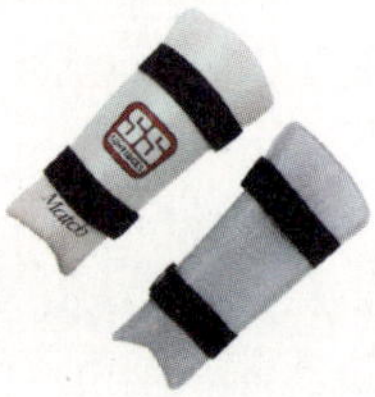

Teaching tips

- Stress on the importance of rules and why they are made.
- Tell students about the consequences of not following rules.
- To substantiate, use examples from daily life.

2. Proud Kuru

Discuss

Look at the pictures. Talk about them in class.

Read along

Kuru the kangaroo is the fastest runner in the forest. He wins all the races. He is proud and does not respect anyone in the forest. None of the other animals like him because of his pride.

Kuru teases Popo the penguin the most. Popo is slow and often cannot even finish a race.

Mozzie the fox is in charge of the races. If animals want to race each other, they tell Mozzie. He tells them the track they can race on.

One day, Kuru asks Popo to race with him. They go to Mozzie. Mozzie, like the other animals, wants to teach Kuru to be humble. He sets the race track over the hill and into the lake. The race finishes on the other side of the lake.

All the animals of the forest come to see the race. 'The one who reaches the finish line first will be the winner,' says Mozzie.

Mozzie counts, '3, 2, 1, Go!' and the race starts. Kuru happily climbs the hill in big leaps and jumps into the lake. Once in the lake, Kuru struggles. He cannot swim very well.

On the other hand, Popo waddles slowly over the hill. When she reaches the water, she jumps right in and swims to the other side of the lake in no time. Kuru is still flapping his hands, legs and tail in the water. He knows how to swim, but cannot swim as fast as Popo.

At last, Kuru reaches the other bank. He is sure that Popo will make fun of him. Instead, Popo smiles and says, 'Dear Kuru, we are friends.'

Think and Say

Your best friend cannot come to your birthday party as her pet dog is sick and she is sad. How would you feel?

Mozzie adds, 'Kuru, this time Popo won the race as she is a good swimmer. You see, everybody is good at something.' Kuru is no longer so proud. He hangs his head and promises to respect everyone.

Figure out

Tick (✓) the correct options to complete the sentences.

1. Kuru ran the fastest, so he was
   a. proud. ☐ b. humble. ☐
2. Popo was slow, but she
   a. respected Kuru. ☐ b. hated Kuru. ☐
3. Mozzie did not like
   a. Popo's pride. ☐ b. Kuru's pride. ☐
4. When Kuru reached the other side, he was sure that Popo would
   a. make fun of him. ☐ b. dance with him. ☐
5. Popo taught Kuru
   a. to respect everyone. ☐ b. to swim. ☐

Relate

Choose the best answer. Draw a smiley ☺ against it.

1. Your friend has shared a secret with you. She asks you not to tell anybody. What would you do?

a. Tell everyone her secret

b. Respect her wish and keep the secret to yourself

2. Your friend's grandmother is not well. Your friend is sad and does not want to go out and play. What would you do?

a. Respect his wish and not force him to play

b. Force him to play with you

3. You have a small quarrel with your friend. Both of you are angry with each other. What would you do the next day?

a. Wait for her to say sorry to you

b. Go to her and say sorry first

Create

1. Make a friendship band for your friend. Here's how you can do it.
   - Cut a strip of coloured paper the size of your wrist.
   - Decorate it with your and your friend's name.

2. Make and give friendship cards to your friends. Complete this sentence and write it on each card.

   I love you because ____

   ____

   ____

Remember

- Respect your friend.
- Say sorry when you are wrong.
- Try to know more about your friends' likes and dislikes.
- Do not behave rudely with your friends.
- Help your friends whenever you can.

Enjoy

Watch the movies *Toy Story, Lion King* and *Tarzan.* Talk about them in class.

Be smart

Observe how your friends behave. Write down two good things that each of them do and try to do them yourself too.

Teaching tips

- Differentiate between pride and arrogance.
- Stress on the strengths of each student.
- Bring out points of strength shown by the characters in the movies listed.

3. Paul and the Picnic

Discuss

Look at the pictures. Talk about them in class.

Read along

Paul woke up late every day. He took a lot of time to bathe and dress and was always late to the breakfast table. He would never reach school on time. His teacher scolded him for being late. But Paul did not care.

One day, Paul's teacher told the class that they were to go for a picnic from school the next day. Paul was very excited! He loved picnics. Paul's teacher told everyone to reach the school at 8:00 a.m. The bus would leave exactly at 8:15 a.m. Knowing that Paul was always late, his teacher told him, especially, to be punctual.

Paul asked his mother to wake him on time. Next morning, his mother woke him. As usual, he did not get up and was late. Even though his father dropped him to school, he reached only at 8:20 a.m. By then, the bus had left with all his classmates and there was nobody in his class.

Think and Say

Your alarm clock has stopped working. How can you still wake up on time?

Paul was very sad. He returned home crying. His mother made him sit on her lap. She wiped his tears and then spoke to him gently. 'Paul, this has happened because you have made it a habit to be late. What do you think you should do?' She asked.

'Mother, I know it is my fault. I promise you and myself that I will never be late again,' he said.

From that day onwards, Paul got up early every morning. He was never late for school again.

Figure out

Tick (✓) the correct options to complete the sentences.

1. When Paul woke up late
   a. he reached school late and was scolded by his teachers. ☐
   b. he could not attend lessons. ☐
2. Paul missed the picnic because
   a. he could not reach school on time. ☐
   b. he did not want to go for the picnic. ☐
3. Paul was sad because
   a. he did not do well in his subjects. ☐
   b. he missed the picnic. ☐

4. What did Paul realize?
   a. He realized that he should make it a habit to be on time. ☐
   b. He realized that missing lessons is a good habit. ☐
5. At the end, Paul changed his habit. List four good things that would have happened to Paul had he always been on time.
   a. ____________________
   b. ____________________
   c. ____________________
   d. ____________________

Relate

Choose the best answer. Draw a smiley ☺ against it.

1. Your friend and you are supposed to go for a birthday party. Your friend is late. What would you do?

a. Get angry and shout at him

b. Help him understand why it is important to be on time

2. Your friend misses classes because he is late and asks for your notebook to take down the notes. What would you do?

a. Do not give him the notebook

b. Give him the notebook and make him promise not to be late again

3. You are late for a movie with your friends. Because of this everybody misses the movie. Your friends get angry. What would you do?

a. Ignore my friends

b. Say sorry to my friends

Create

Following a timetable is very important. Make a clock with your daily routine and hang it in your room. Follow it strictly to ensure that you are never late for anything.

You need

- A sheet of coloured chart paper
- Scissors
- Coloured markers
- Ribbon
- Compass

Steps

1. Draw a big circle on the chart paper and cut it out.
2. Divide the circle into 24 equal parts.
3. Write the time and the activity that you do in that time slot in the different parts of the circle.
4. Decorate it as you like.
5. Fold the ribbon in a loop and paste it at the back of the circle.

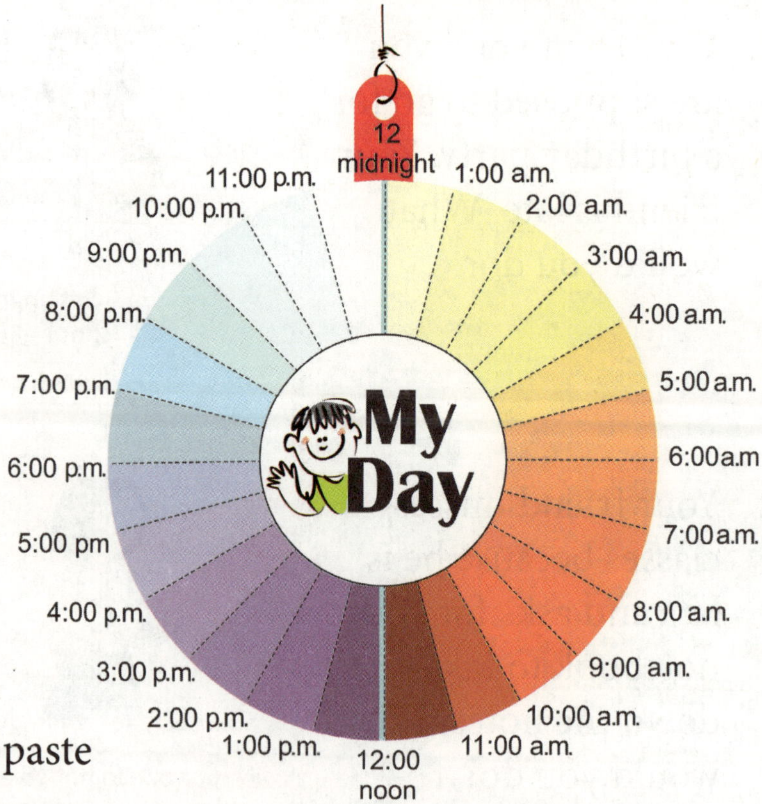

Hang it in your room and follow it every day.

Remember

- Get up early.
- Plan a daily timetable and follow it.
- Pack your bag according to the class timetable before going to bed.
- Keep your school dress on a hanger with shoes and socks ready before going to bed.
- Set your clock ahead of time by 5–10 minutes. This will help you to be on time.

Enjoy

Read the story *Black and White* about being on time. You could look up the Internet to find the story.

Be smart

1. Arrange these ten words related to time in alphabetical order.

second	hour	calendar	clock	year
minute	day	month	week	time

1. ____________ 2. ____________

3. ____________ 4. ____________

5. ____________ 6. ____________

7. ____________ 8. ____________

9. ____________ 10. ____________

2. Here is a game that you and your friends can play with your teacher to practise completing work on time.

   Divide your class into teams of four children each. Your teacher will give you a number of cards with the letters of the alphabet on them. Your teacher will also give you a time limit. Make as many words as you can using all the letter cards.

   The team which makes the most number of correct words, in the time given, wins the game.

3. Observe people around you. Make a list of activities and people who follow a set time for work.

   ______________________ ______________________

   ______________________ ______________________

   ______________________ ______________________

   ______________________ ______________________

   ______________________ ______________________

Teaching tips

- Tell students how being late affects the schedule of other people.
- Stress on how so many other people have to be on time so that students can attend classes.
- Talk about how students' parents have to leave for work or get up on time.
- Give examples of activities and people who follow a set timetable for work.

4. Holly Loves Lavender

Discuss

Look at the pictures. Talk about them in class.

Read along

Holly was a rabbit who loved lavender. She loved its smell, its taste and even its colour. Wherever she found lavender, she would start munching it. Holly ate so much lavender that she became really big. Soon, she was the biggest rabbit in the burrow. But she couldn't stop eating lavender.

The other rabbits in the burrow began to worry. Lavender was vanishing from their gardens. Holly ate it all. Lavender was not just food for the rabbits. Lavender was a herb. It was medicine to cure sick rabbits, too.

Soon, some rabits from the burrow fell sick. But there was no lavender to cure them. What would happen now?

Holly became sad. She had been greedy and eaten up all the lavender. She did not think that it would take so much time for the lavender plants to grow back.

One day, Holly saw a small sprig of lavender in the forest. She had not eaten any lavender for weeks. She wanted so much to bite into the sweet smelling leaves. But she remembered the rabbits who were ill. She carefully cleared the ground around the tiny plant and watered it. Every day she cared for it. Soon it grew tall and other tiny lavender plants started growing around it too.

When the rabbits got to know, they thanked Holly. They took a few leaves from each plant and fed them to the sick rabbits. Holly was happy she could help others.

Think and Say

You notice that your younger sister does not switch off the lights of the room when she leaves. What would you do?

Figure out

Tick (✓) the correct options to answer the questions.

1. Do you think it was right for Holly to eat all the lavender?
   a. Yes, because she liked it. ☐
   b. No, because she didn't leave any for others. ☐
2. What happened when there wasn't any lavender left for the other rabbits?
   a. They could not be cured once they fell ill. ☐
   b. They were happy. ☐
3. Holly took care of the lavender plant she found. Why do you think she did this?
   a. Holly felt sad about her actions in the past and wanted to make things right. ☐
   b. She wanted to eat more lavender. ☐

4. If Holly knew what her actions would lead to, would she have eaten all the lavender?
   a. Yes. ☐
   b. No. ☐
5. Do you think that Holly will eat all the lavender ever again?
   a. Yes, because it is tasty. ☐
   b. No, because she has seen what the result can be. ☐

Relate

Choose the best answer. Draw a smiley ☺ against it.

1. If you see a man cutting a tree in your backyard, what would you do?

a. Let him cut it down

b. Call your mother to ask the man to stop cutting the tree

2. If you saw a baby plant growing in your garden, what would you do?

a. Water it to help the plant grow

b. Not care whether it grew or not

3. If you heard a hungry kitten outside your home, what would you do?

a. Leave the kitten alone

b. Give the kitten some food

Create

Go to your garden at school or at home and collect a few fallen flowers and leaves. Paste these on a large, coloured chart paper. Find out the names of the plants from the gardener. Write the names under each flower and leaf. Display your garden chart in your room.

Remember

- All plants and animals are our friends.
- Never hurt plants or animals.
- Never pluck flowers or tear leaves.
- Don't waste paper. Paper comes from trees and wasting paper means killing trees.
- If you see a running tap, turn it off.

Enjoy

Watch the movie *Finding Nemo* and notice the beautiful undersea environment shown in the movie.

Be smart

Have you seen an LED bulb? Do you know that an LED bulb is good for the environment? Find out the full form of LED and how it is good for the environment. Make a scrapbook page on this. Display it in the class.

Teaching tips

- Bring out the unexpected dangers of Holly's actions.
- Tell children about how electricity and environment are connected.
- Talk to the children about the environment in totality, that is, including oceans, underground environment, forests and space.

5. Grandfather's Little Mother

Discuss

Look at the pictures. Talk about them in class.

Read along

Sukhi was visiting her grandfather during the vacation. Her grandfather was a farmer.

Grandfather and Sukhi would get up very early. They had many things to do on the farm. Grandfather would milk the cow. Sukhi would gather the eggs from the coop. Grandfather would cook breakfast. Sukhi would feed hay to the cows and grain to the hens.

Think and Say

You see that your father is washing the car. What would you do?

Then Sukhi would go to play and Grandfather would go to the fields. When Grandfather returned, they would have lunch. After some rest, both of them would go around the farm again. They had to see that the animals were resting.

At night, Grandfather would tell Sukhi stories till they both fell asleep.

One morning, Grandfather fell ill. When Sukhi saw that he was not feeling well, she tucked him in his bed. She said, 'Grandfather, please rest. Today, I will take care of your chores and all the animals.'

Grandfather groaned, 'That's a lot of work, Sukhi! You will not be able to manage all this on your own.'

Sukhi shook her head. 'Grandfather, you cared for me. You always looked after me when I was sick. Now it is my turn,' she said patting his hand.

Grandfather smiled and lay back on his pillows.

Sukhi ran around the farm doing everything she could. She also took care of Grandfather. She fed him hot soup. By that evening, Grandfather felt better.

Grandfather said, 'Sukhi, you have become my little mother.' Sukhi just smiled and asked him to rest.

Later, Grandfather told everyone, 'My Sukhi is the best granddaughter I could ever have.'

—*Sutapa Basu*

Figure out

Tick (✓) the correct options to answer the questions.

1. Why did Sukhi run around the farm doing everything she could?
   a. Because Sukhi hated the work on the farm. ☐
   b. Because Sukhi had a lot of work to complete and she had to take care of Grandfather as well. ☐
2. Should Grandfather have forced himself to get up and do the work?
   a. Yes. He was not too ill. ☐
   b. No. It is better to take rest when you are ill so that you recover quickly. ☐
3. Should Sukhi have left the work of the farm for the next day?
   a. No. Sukhi did the right thing by helping her Grandfather. ☐
   b. Yes. It is all right for work to be left for the next day. ☐
4. Why did Grandfather call Sukhi his little mother?
   a. Because Sukhi showed love and care, and helped Grandfather just like mothers do. ☐
   b. Because she did the work on the farm, just like mothers do.
5. Do you think Sukhi should have been rewarded for helping Grandfather?
   a. Yes. After all, she did extra work. ☐
   b. No. Helping others is a selfless act. ☐

Relate

Choose the best answer. Draw a smiley ☺ against it.

1. If you see a friend has missed school because she was ill, and there is a test coming up, what would you do?

a. Let her be as she is

b. Help her study for the test

2. You see a blind man walking on the pavement. He is about to walk into a lamp post. What would you do?

a. Let him walk on

b. Help him immediately

3. You see a book drop out of a lady's bag. Not knowing about it, she walks on. What would you do?

a. Pick up the book, run up to her and return it

b. Let the book be on the road

Create

Make cards for three people who helped you in the past week. Decorate them and write 'Thank you for your help' on them. Inside the card, write a short note to the person.

Remember

- Helping people has its own rewards.
- You can make someone very happy by helping them.
- Always look out for ways in which you can help someone in need.
- Small good deeds matter a lot. Try to do them on a daily basis.

Enjoy

Watch the film *Superman*. See how Superman uses his powers to help all those in need without asking them for anything in return.

Be smart

Match the following helpful actions with the pictures.

Helping a friend with the lessons he missed because he was unwell.

Helping Mother and Father lay the table.

Helping a friend carry his bag.

Helping your younger sister clean her cupboard.

Teaching tips

- Stress on how personalities like Mother Teresa helped others selflessly.
- Tell the students that when they help someone in need without expecting anything in return, it is a selfless act.
- Tell students about the circle of help—that help always comes back twofold when least expected, but most needed.

Life Skills: Bus Manners

A school bus is our own school property. We must take care of how we behave in it. We should not make it dirty or damage it.

Here is a list of things that we should and should not do in the bus.

What we should do while travelling in a school bus:

- We should talk quietly amongst ourselves.
- We should not disturb the driver.
- We should keep our bags and other things with ourselves.
- We should listen to the person in charge of the bus.

What we should not do while travelling in a school bus:

- We should not run or jump about.
- We should not hang from the safety rail.
- We should not pull or push one another.
- We should not try to scare other people travelling in the bus.
- We should not throw fruit peels, empty chips packets or any other things out of the window of the bus.
- We should not make the window or the seats of the bus dirty by writing on them.
- We should not scream in the bus and disturb others.

How Do you Come to School?

Conduct a class survey. Ask your classmates how they come to school. Tick (✓) the right column according to your classmates' answers.

Results

Number of children who come by bus ______________

Number of children who come by car ______________

Number of children who come by bicycle ______________

Number of children who walk to school ______________

Going alone to school is no fun, but in a carpool the sport would have just begun.

Colour the poster. Circle the pictures that show children misbehaving in the bus.

Project I: Make a Green Guide

Look around your neighbourhood. Are there any places where you can find different plants and smell the scents of flowers? Make a list of all such places. You can include places like parks, flower shops, plant nurseries and so on. Draw a picture of each place and write in two or three sentences about what you have seen there. Then display your guide in class.

6. Rats! Rats! Rats!

Discuss

Look at the pictures. Talk about them in class.

Read along

Little Aimol loved playing pranks.

He would tease everyone and play pranks on them. He would also lie to his family. He would scare his sister by saying, 'Look at the rats under your bed! They will bite you at night.' His sister would get scared and cry.

One day, his grandmother was boiling soup. Aimol took a spoonful and said, 'Yuck! No salt.' His grandmother mixed some more salt into it though she had, in fact, put salt in it earlier. That evening, nobody could have the salty soup!

Another day, he told his father, 'Dad, your car has been stolen!' His dad ran out instantly. The car was found right in the middle of their driveway. Inside the house, Aimol was rolling on the carpet, laughing so hard that his stomach hurt.

One night, Grandfather decided to tell him the story of the shepherd boy who played a prank by shouting, 'Wolf! Wolf!'

'So, when the wolf really came, and the boy shouted "wolf", nobody believed him,' said Grandfather. But Aimol only laughed when Grandfather finished the story, and went off to sleep.

Think and Say

Your friend is asking you to play a prank on another friend. What would you do?

That night, something strange happened. Aimol heard some screeching noises and woke up with a startle. It was dark. The noises were coming from under his bed. He peeped

and was horrified! There were rats and rats and rats under his bed. He shouted, 'Mum! Dad! Rats! Rats!' But, nobody came.

Aimol jumped from his bed and ran to the living room. Everyone sat there, chatting. He said, 'Come quickly! There are rats under my bed!' Nobody even looked at him. Aimol shouted again, 'I am not lying. Please believe me!' Nobody even bothered to get up.

'Aimol! Aimol!' called someone. Aimol opened his eyes. It was Grandfather.

Aimol sat up. 'The rats?' he said.

'What rats?' his grandfather asked, 'You were shouting in your sleep. Did you have a bad dream?'

'So all those rats were a dream!' Aimol sighed with relief. From that day, Aimol decided never to tell lies again. And, never did he play pranks on anyone to trouble them either.

Figure out

Tick (✓) the correct options to answer the questions.

1. Do you think scaring someone as a prank is fun?
   a. Yes. It is fun! ☐
   b. No. It is not fun. ☐
2. Do you think Aimol could have found a better way to spend his time?
   a. No. Playing pranks is a good hobby. ☐
   b. Yes. Aimol could have spent his time more wisely. He could have read books or painted pictures or even learnt to play an instrument. ☐
3. Do you think that Aimol's dream actually taught him a lesson?
   a. Yes. Aimol needed to realize that lying is bad. ☐
   b. No. Aimol continued to play pranks. ☐

4. Do you think Grandfather told the story of the boy who cried 'Wolf!' to Aimol on purpose?
   a. Yes. So that Aimol could learn from the story. ☐
   b. No. He just told him a story. ☐
5. Do you think Aimol will play more pranks in future?
   a. Yes. I think so. ☐
   b. No. I do not think so. ☐

Relate

Choose the best answer. Draw a smiley ☺ against it.

1. When you were playing cricket, the ball you hit broke your father's windscreen. What would you do?

a. Confess to Father about the windscreen

b. Hide and lie to him if he asks

2. Last night, you were sleepy and could not finish your homework. What would you tell your teacher?

a. Lie to your teacher and tell her that you were ill

b. Tell your teacher the truth

3. You have broken your brother's toy. What would you do?

a. Tell him that you broke his toy, and say sorry

b. Hide the broken toy

Create

Find a poem on being honest. Write it on a piece of chart paper. Hang it in your room. Read it every day and remind yourself to have a truthful day ahead.

Remember

- Lying is a bad habit.
- Lying can hurt people.
- If you always lie, no one will believe you when you speak the truth.
- Being truthful is a good quality. We must practise it.

Enjoy

Read the story *The Boy Who Cried Wolf!* Discuss the story in class.

Be smart

Write two words that mean the opposite of the words 'lie' and 'truth'.

Lie	Truth
______________	______________
______________	______________

Teaching tips

- Tell the students about the concepts of honesty and dishonesty, and include examples such as cheating and bribing.
- Stress on ways to make better use of time, such as working on a hobby.
- Tell the students about the rewards and consequences of being honest and dishonest. Tell them that we are responsible for the results of our actions.

7. The Fish Unite

Discuss

Look at the pictures. Talk about them in class.

Read along

Deep in the forest was a big river. All kinds of fish lived in the river. Each group of fish was different. No group was friendly with the other group.

All the groups lived and played separately. The elder fish kept telling the younger fish to remain together and united. But the younger fish did not listen to them.

One day, a big fish, by the name of Sim, came into the river. She started eating the small fish one by one. Every day some fish from each group went missing.

'What is happening? Why are our numbers decreasing every day?' asked a fish one day.

'I think Sim is eating our brothers and sisters,' replied another fish.

Concerned, all the groups of fish went to their elders.

'Please help us or Sim will eat us all up,' said one small fish.

'This was the reason we had told you to be united,' said the elder fish.

'Now listen carefully and do as we say,' said another elder.

The younger fish listened carefully and understood the plan.

The next day when Sim came to eat the small fish, she saw a much bigger fish than herself.

All the small fish groups had united to make one large fish. Swimming together they looked like a very large fish.

Sim was very frightened. She swam fast for her life as the large fish chased her. She left the river as fast as she could and never came back again.

'Hurray!' the younger fish cheered. They celebrated their unity.

'Now do you see how unity helps? When all of you unite to face danger, you win,' said the elders.

'Oh yes! From now on, we will always remain united,' said all the younger fish.

Think and Say

Your mother is not well today. How can your brother and you work together and show that you love and care for your mother?

Figure out

Tick (✓) the correct options to complete the sentences.

1. The different groups of fish living in the river were
   a. friendly with each other. ☐ b. unfriendly with each other. ☐
2. The elder fish asked the younger fish to
   a. remain united. ☐ b. fight among themselves. ☐
3. Sim was able to eat the small fish because
   a. they were naughty. ☐ b. they were not united. ☐
4. To get rid of Sim, all the small fish
   a. united together. ☐ b. left the stream. ☐
5. Sim swam away because
   a. she was a coward. ☐ b. the small fish had united. ☐

Relate

Choose the best answer. Draw a smiley ☺ against it.

1. Only a few students of your class get selected for the annual play competition. What should the others do?

a. Unite and help them prepare for it

b. Stop talking to them

2. Your friend's cycle is stuck in the mud and he is unable to take it out. What would you do?

a. Leave him there and go away

b. Help him to take the cycle out

3. You and your friends play in the park every day. One day, some older boys tell you to leave the park for them to play. What would you do?

a. Quietly leave the park

b. Get together and discuss how both the groups can play

Create

All of us have large families with aunts, uncles and cousins. We meet the family over weekends or during celebrations. Together we go for picnics, holidays or parties.

Let's make a family team with all our cousins. Give the team a nice name.

Just as every sports team has a uniform, your family's team also needs a uniform. Let us make this team uniform (a T-shirt) for everybody.

You need

- A coloured T-shirt for each cousin (Choose any one colour)
- Fabric paint

Steps

1. Take the T-shirt.
2. With the help of an adult, write the name of the team on the T-shirt.
3. Using fabric colours, decorate the T-shirt.

You can wear this T-shirt at the next family get together and also gift these to your other cousins.

Remember

- In school, you can show unity by taking part in all activities.
- You can show unity at home by helping with the housework.
- You can show unity among friends by playing a game that everyone likes.

Enjoy

Watch the movie *Turbo.* Discuss in class how unity was displayed in the movie.

Be smart

Tommy is lost in the maze. Help Timmy find Tommy so that they can have lunch with their mother.

Teaching tips

- Stress on the benefits of being united in class.
- Give more examples of unity from life.
- Make students aware of the difference between right and wrong—unity for a good cause and unity to create mischief.

8. The Puppet Show

Discuss

Look at the pictures. Talk about them in class.

Cooperation

Read along

One day, our teacher, Renu Ma'am divided the drama class into groups. There were three children in each group. She wanted each group to put up a play.

Radha, Azim and Jassi were in one group.

'I cannot act,' said Jassi.

'Neither can I,' said Azim.

'That's okay, I can act,' Radha volunteered.

'But how will we do the play together?' Radha asked.

Azim had an idea. 'Why don't we put up a puppet show?' He told Jassi, 'Jassi, you are good at craft. So, why don't you make the puppets? I am good at games, so I'll take care of the puppet show.'

'And I am good at acting, so I'll say the dialogues,' Radha added.

'Wow! This sounds great!' Jassi said happily.

All the three started doing what they were good at.

In no time, Jassi made the puppets, Radha wrote and rehearsed her

Think and Say

Your father wants to take you and your friend for a movie. But your friend falls sick. What would you do?

dialogues, while Azim planned out the show.

When it was time for them to perform, everything was ready and in place. With Jassi's puppets, Radha's dialogues and Azim's planning, the three friends put up a great puppet show.

As their play ended, Renu Ma'am clapped and said, 'I am very happy with this group's play. Each student did what he or she is good at and made the play a success. This is real cooperation. Jassi, Azim and Radha are the winners.'

All the students clapped, while Radha, Jassi and Azim stood together and beamed with happiness.

Figure out

Tick (✓) the correct options to complete the sentences.

1. The drama class was divided into groups of
   a. three children each. ☐
   b. two children each. ☐
2. Radha, Jassi and Azim's group presented a
   a. dance show. ☐
   b. puppet show. ☐

3. Radha, Jassi and Azim decided to
   a. cooperate with each other. ☐
   b. give up trying to put up a play. ☐
4. The three children worked as a team. Each one did what they were
   a. good at. ☐
   b. not good at. ☐
5. Radha, Jassi and Azim were winners because
   a. they cooperated with each other. ☐
   b. they fought with each other. ☐

Relate

Choose the best answer. Draw a smiley ☺ against it.

1. Your friend and you have to make a picture chart for the class together. What would you do?

a. Divide the work and complete the project

b. Fight with your friend

2. You have come to play with your cousin, but she has to finish making her scrapbook. What would you do?

a. Help her make the scrapbook

b. Do not help her and complain of being bored

3. The children in your class are participating in a pyramid competition. What would you do?

a. Do not participate in the competition

b. Enjoy participating in the competition

Create

Firefighters, cricketers and footballers need to work as a team in order to get their jobs done. Think of some other types of jobs that need a group of people to work together. Write these down on a coloured chart paper. Write three ways in which each member helps the team.

Remember

- You can cooperate with friends by sharing responsibilities.
- Cooperation doesn't mean that you do your friend's homework.
- Sometimes, play games that your friends like, instead of games that you like.

Enjoy

Watch the film *Madagascar*. Discuss it in the class.

Be smart

1. Play this game in groups of four.

Ball on the Blanket
How to play:
a. Each group is given a blanket.

b. Each person will hold the four corners of the blanket.

c. Place a ball in the centre of the blanket.

d. On the 'GO' signal, you have to work together to throw the ball off the blanket and into the air.

e. Then, you have to catch the ball on its way back down.

f. The team that makes the maximum number of bounces and catches, within a particular time, wins the game.

2. Write the first letters of these phrases to get a new word.

Get along ◯

Respect others ◯

Obey rules ◯

Use low voices ◯

Participate ◯

Got the new word? Write it here.

__ __ __ __ __

What does this word mean to you? Discuss in class.

Teaching tips

- Make the students aware of the importance of working in teams.
- Stress that trusting others is important for teamwork.
- Tell students about how teams are built around individual strengths.

9. The Crow Who Showed Off

Discuss

Look at the pictures. Talk about them in class.

Read along

Once in a forest there lived a group of crows. One crow among them was stronger than the rest. His name was Rex.

Rex could fly higher and faster than all the crows. He always boasted that he knew one hundred and one ways of flying. The other crows were very impressed and made him their king. Soon, he became King Rex, an arrogant bird.

One day, from a land far away, an eagle came to the forest. His name was Aquila. The crows saw Aquila flying in the sky. They were impressed by the manner in which he was flying. When he landed, they gathered around him.

They boasted about King Rex to Aquila. One crow said, 'Our king is the greatest.'

Another crow said, 'Yes, he knows a lot of different ways of flying. He is truly great!' The other crows then cawed loudly cheering Rex.

Though Aquila was simple and wise, he was quite taken aback by the crows' praise of their king. Hearing about the glory of King Rex, Aquila expressed his wish to meet him. He asked, 'May I have the honour of meeting King Rex?'

The crows happily led him to meet King Rex. Aquila bowed low before King Rex and said, 'I am grateful to have met you, O Great king!'

The king asked, 'How many ways can you fly?'

The wise Aquila was surprised. He said, 'I know only one way to fly, O king!'

King Rex puffed his chest and said, 'I know one hundred and one ways of flying. Let me show you some.' Then he went on to show Aquila his acrobatic flying.

Think and Say

Would you admit that you don't know an answer in class?

Finally, when King Rex landed, he said, 'Now Aquila, you show me your way.'

Eagles fly very high and very fast. So Aquila rose slowly and easily into the sky. King Rex went along too. Then Aquila gathered speed and flew even higher. Soon he was soaring in the sky and flying very, very fast. King Rex was only a crow. He could not keep up with the skill of an eagle. As he struggled to fly alongside Aquila, he fell into the sea.

The arrogant king was about to drown. In the nick of time, Aquila dived down and saved King Rex. He picked up King Rex with his strong claws and took him back to the forest.

As King Rex recovered, he realized his foolishness. Humbled, by Aquila's skill and modesty, King Rex was never arrogant about his flying again. Soon the modest Aquila and the humbled king became good friends.

Figure out

Tick (✓) the correct options to answer the questions.

1. Why do you think the other crows made Rex their king?
   a. They were impressed by how strong Rex was. ☐
   b. They were scared of how strong Rex was. ☐
2. Why do you think King Rex was foolish?
   a. He was proud of something that did not make him a better king. ☐
   b. He had to take help from Aquila. ☐
3. How do you know that Aquila was simple and wise?
   a. Aquila did not show off even though he was a better flyer. ☐
   b. Aquila also thought that the crow should be the king. ☐
4. What led to King Rex's downfall?
   a. His pride and that he showed off. ☐
   b. His simplicity. ☐
5. Could King Rex's one hundred and one ways of flying help him in any way?
   a. Yes. ☐ b. No. ☐

Relate

Choose the best answer. Draw a smiley ☺ against it.

1. If someone tries to put you down by showing off their latest video game, what would you do?

a. Listen quietly and not show off in return

b. Ask your father to get one so that you can show off too

2. Your neighbour has bought a new cricket set and shows it off. How would you feel?

a. Jealous

b. Happy for him

3. Your father has got you a new bicycle. It looks smart and pretty. Which of these would you do?

a. Brag about it to all my friends

b. Allow my friends to ride it too

Create

Make a poster of this poem. Decorate it with colourful pictures. Display it in the class.

Little Things

Little drops of water,
Little grains of sand,
Make the mighty ocean,
And the pleasant land.
Thus the little minutes,
Humble though they be,
Make the mighty ages,
Of eternity.

—Ebenezer Cobham Brewer

Remember

- Be humble.
- Be happy with the little joys you have in life.
- Be happy with the little actions you do in life.
- Share your things with everyone.
- Do not show off what you have.
- Do not compare yourself with others.
- Do not demand things that others have.

Enjoy

Read the book *The Rianbow Fish* by Marcus Pfister. You can find this book in your school library. You can also look for this book on the Internet.

Be smart

What is wrong with the picture below? Write in the space provided.

Teaching tips

- Talk about the concept of humility.
- Stress on the difference between humility and low self esteem.
- Ask students to give examples of humility from daily life.

10. Carrots and Cabbage, Please

Discuss

Look at the pictures. Talk about them in class.

Read along

Sid did not want to wake up on the first day of his holidays. He had to go with his parents to visit his grandparents at their farm for a week. Sid loved his grandparents dearly, but he would not get his favourite brand of chips outside the city. How could he live without chips! So, in his tiny bag, Sid filled packets and packets of his favourite chips.

At the farm, he greeted his grandmother, grandfather and their dog, Scrappy. While his parents and grandparents chatted, Sid quietly went out of the room. Carefully, he took a handful of chips from his bag and gobbled them up. Then he ran out to play.

Sid munched chips all through the day. So, he was never hungry at mealtimes. He said no to porridge, no to milk, no to carrots and no to beans.

Something else also happened. He felt tired all the time. If he ran with Scrappy, he became breathless and wanted to sit down.

After two days of gobbling chips, Sid had no more chips. What would he eat now!

'Chips are junk food, Sid. How long will you not eat real food?' Grandfather said.

Finally, his grandmother said, 'Search for potatoes in the vegetable patch, Sid. If you find any, I will

make chips for you.' Sid happily picked up a large basket and went to the vegetable patch.

Think and Say

You are hungry for a snack. In the kitchen, you find a packet of your favourite biscuits and two apples. Which of these will you eat and why?

Sid searched and searched but found no potatoes. Tired and sulky, he walked into Grandmother's kitchen with a basket full of carrots and a cabbage.

At dinner, Sid saw some green leaves on a plate, an orange jelly in a bowl, a cool orange juice, orange chips and some warm orange drink in another bowl.

Sid wanted to know what they were. Grandmother said, 'The green leaves are fried cabbage. The orange jelly is carrot *halwa*, the orange juice is carrot juice, the orange chips are, of course, carrot chips and the warm orange drink in the bowl is a carrot and cabbage soup.'

One by one, Sid tasted each. His mouth started curling into a wide grin. He could not believe that carrots and cabbage tasted even better than chips!

He had carrots and cabbage for the rest of the week. He was never tired again.

Figure out

Tick (✓) the correct options to complete the sentences.

1. Sid did not want to go to his grandparents' farm because
   a. he did not like them. ☐
   b. he would not get his favourite brand of chips there. ☐
2. Sid did not eat at mealtimes because
   a. he had eaten chips and was not hungry. ☐
   b. his grandmother had scolded him. ☐
3. Sid felt tired because
   a. he ate chips all the time. ☐
   b. he was sick. ☐
4. Sid happily went to the vegetable patch
   a. to search for potatoes. ☐
   b. to search for carrots. ☐
5. When Sid ate carrots and cabbages every day, he felt
   a. happy and active. ☐
   b. tired and breathless. ☐

Relate

Choose the best answer. Draw a smiley ☺ against it.

1. You have got cucumber sandwiches for your school break. You do not like them. What would you do?

◯ 

a. Eat the sandwiches as they are healthy

◯ 

b. Buy a burger from the school canteen as it is tastier

2. There is a school fete and you have ten rupees to buy a snack. What will you buy?

a. Mixed vegetable pulao

b. Chips and cola

3. You want to call your friends home for lunch. Your mother says she will cook a meal for your friends. What will you say to your mother?

a. You will thank her for the meal for your friends

b. You will say that you want to order pizzas for your friends

Create

Follow these steps to make a delicious cucumber sandwich.

You need

- Two slices of bread
- Butter
- 4 cucumber slices (Ask an elder person to slice the cucumber.)

Steps

1. Keep the two slices of bread on a plate.
2. Spread butter on both the slices.
3. Place the cucumber slices on one bread slice.
4. Cover it with the other slice and press down.
5. Your delicious cucumber sandwich is ready.

Remember

We must eat lots of healthy food because

- it gives us energy.
- it does not let us fall ill.
- it builds our bones and muscles.
- it repairs our bodies when we fall ill.

We must eat very little junk food because

- it does not give us any of the things that healthy food gives us.
- it can make us sick.

Enjoy

Find and read these stories from your school library. You could also find them on the Internet.

1. *Reggie Mouse's Shrinking Clothes*
2. *The Very Hungry Caterpillar*
3. *The Burger who did not Want to be Junk Food*

Be Smart

Can you guess the names of these fruits and vegetables?

1. Which vegetable comes in layers and can make you cry?
2. Which fruit is the same colour as its name?
3. Which vegetable grows under the ground and has eyes?
4. Which summer fruit is big and green outside and red and juicy inside?
5. Which juicy fruit can be eaten whole and in slices, drunk as a juice and cooked into pickles and chutneys?

Teaching tips

- Tell the students about different foods that give us energy, help repair damaged body parts, build bones and muscles.
- You may draw the food pyramid which the children would be learning in EVS or Science.
- Talk about common foods that can become tasty when cooked in certain ways.
- Stress on eating more healthy food and less junk food.

Project II: The Mystery Box

Six people can play this game at one go.

Make teams of three each. Name the teams A and B.

Take an old shoe box with a lid. This can be made into a mystery box.

Group A places some things in the box. Make sure Group B does not see them.

Groups A and B have to stand facing each other. Place the mystery box in the centre, between the two groups.

Let one person from Group A describe a thing that has been placed in the box by giving examples and talking about it. The person has to be careful not to say the name of the thing. The person from Group B, standing in the opposite direction, will have to guess the thing.

For example, if Marie of Group A has placed a toy plane inside the box, she may say:

It flies in the sky.

We can go from one place to another in it.

Continue playing the game till all the members of the groups have had a chance. Only three hints are allowed. If the child from Group B cannot guess the object in three hints, it means that the two students need to work on cooperating and try again at a later date.

At the end, judge how many pairs could cooperate well to complete the task.

Notes

Notes

Notes

Notes

Notes

Notes